# BIRMINGHAM BACK TO THE SEVENTIES

### Alton & Jo Douglas

Christ Church Passage (with New Street in view) 1970. Shortly after this picture was taken the buildings on the right were demolished.

© 2007 Alton and Jo Douglas
ISBN 978-1-85858-410-2
Published by Brewin Books Ltd., Doric House, 56 Alcester Road, Studley, Warwickshire B80 7LG.
Printed by Warwick Printing Co. Ltd., Theatre Street, Warwick CV34 4DR.
Layout by Alton and Jo Douglas

Poplar Road, Kings Heath, looking towards High Street, 11th September 1973.

Front Cover: The Council House, Victoria Square, 14th May 1971.

# Contents

# BREWIN BOOKS LTD

Doric House, 56 Alcester Road,
Studley, Warwickshire B80 7LG

Tel: 01527 854228  Fax: 01527 852746

Vat Registration No. 705 0077 73

*Dear Nostalgic,*

*When I was a lad there was a gadget, a bit like a periscope, that enabled you to look over the heads in a crowd. Try and imagine that you're using one to see behind you and you'll notice that the 70's are fading further and further into the distance. Some people refer to the period as "only yesterday" but in reality the decade finished over a quarter of a century ago. So, what have we got for you this time? Scores of streets to stroll along, lots of window-shopping to do and crowds full of faces to look through (and hopefully identify some of them). In total, over 350 items – if you've got the time and energy, just count them. Incidentally, the Queen seemed almost to be addicted to our city, she visited us so often and – as you'll see – how we turned out to greet her on every occasion!*

*Once again, many thanks to all our contributors, with a special mention to Brian Matthews who gave us unfettered access to his unique collection of pictures (Christ Church Passage, Hay Hall, Stratford House, etc.).*

*Our books are often shaped by your comments so do remember that feedback is important to us.*

*Yours, in friendship,*

Alton

Acknowledgements for the Queen, Victoria Square, 27th July 1977.

Smallbrook Ringway, with Hurst Street on the left,
January 1970.

Snow Hill Station is reduced to a car park, c 1970.

**T**HE three Apollo 13 astronauts were fighting for their lives 200,000 miles out in space today after a massive power failure in their spacecraft.

The moon landing was abandoned and the astronauts thrown into grave danger when the electrical system in their spacecraft blew out with a loud bang.

For a few seconds the space vessel spun out of control as warning lights flashed on in the conical command module occupied by 42-year-old James Lovell, Fred Haise and substitute John Swigert, both 38.

Two of Apollo 13's three supply cells, which feed the spaceship its energy, had failed and oxygen was seeping from one cell and the crew cabin space.

Mission Control here abandoned the moon-landing and worked on an emergency plan to bring the astronauts back to earth.

14.4.70

Elizabeth Gourley and Mary Hussain survey the flooding in the backyards of houses in Regent Park Road, Small Heath, 21st April 1970.

Kings Norton Retired Gentlemen's Club, The Green, c 1970.

**A** MAJOR office complex is being planned for Hagley Road, Edgbaston, by Laing Development Company in association with Calthorpe Estates.

An early start on the construction of the block will be made in 1971, and occupation is expected to be possible by the summer of 1972.

The scheme will occupy one of the finest office locations in the West Midlands, on the north side of Hagley Road, which is less than two miles from Birmingham city centre.

Joyce Noxon enjoys her farewell party as she retires as relief matron of Bicknell Croft Children's Home, Druids Heath, 15th May 1970.

Issued by the West Midlands Gas Board.

HOSPITAL

EXIT

OXYGEN

John Wood

Hurry home to High Speed Gas, health and happiness

Just some of the people who left New Street Station for Exmouth to see the launch of the new "City of Birmingham" lifeboat, 16th May 1970.

## Two days to the 'go gay' festival

**Evening Mail Reporter**

City Centre Spring Festival

BIRMINGHAM'S City Centre Spring Festival gets into full swing on Monday.

The first day's programme includes:

9.30 a.m. Park and ride system starts from Bristol Street Spring Vale car park.

10.00 Continuous film shows begin in the conference room at New Street Station.

10.30 Official opening speech by the Lord Mayor, Alderman Neville Bosworth, in the Colmore Circus Beer Garden.

### Balloons

10.35 Release of hundreds of balloons by the Lord Mayor.

10.45 Finalists in the Miss City Centre contest parade for the judges, again in the beer garden.

11.30 Crowning of beauty queen. Beer garden opens for business.

12 Pop group Reflections play in the beer garden.

2.30 Judges out looking for best-dressed women shoppers.

The city's first International Spring Festival, Cannon Hill Park, 18th May 1970.

Temporary road signs show the way, Colmore Row, 1970.

The Lord Mayor and Lady Mayoress, Ald. and Mrs Stanley Bleyer, welcome some of the children taking part in the school service at Birmingham Cathedral, 23rd June 1970.

Hilda Schroder and Michael Cotterill, as the angry parents, get to grips with Paul Henry, in the Alexandra Theatre's production of "Billy Liar", 28th July 1970.

St Stephens Road/Milner Road, Stirchley, 1970.

Manzoni Gardens, Bull Ring, 1970.

Hay Hall, Hay Hall Road, off King's Road, Tyseley, c 1970.

Stratford House, Camp Hill, c 1970.

A classical recital by a quartet from the City of Birmingham Symphony Orchestra, The Opposite Lock, Bridge Street, 15th October 1970. The nightclub normally was home to the sounds of jazz and pop music.

Edgbaston Shopping Centre, Five Ways, 1st December 1970.

The Lord Mayor, Ald. Stanley Bleyer, enjoys the Birmingham Mail's Chipper Club trip to the ABC cinema, Selly Oak, 28th December 1970.

The Town Hall, seen from Waterloo Street, 1970.

St Georges C of E School football team, Newtown, 1970/71.

The Pathology Laboratory ladies' football team, Dudley Road Hospital, 1971.

Coventry Road, with Golden Hillock Road on the left, Small Heath, 1971.

Coventry Road/Muntz Street, Small Heath, 1971.

Sandy Lane, from Camp Hill, Bordesley, 1971.

Congregational Church, Union Row, Grove Lane, Handsworth, 1971.

The Queen meets crowds at Chelmsley Wood,
7th April 1971.

The Queen enjoys a chat during her visit to the city, Colmore Row, 7th April 1971.
She was here to open the Inner Ring Road.

A break, in Holloway Circus, from rehearsals for some of the cast of "Not Now Darling", at the Alexandra Theatre, 26th April 1971.

18

Ansells Brewery, Park Road, Aston Cross, 27th April 1971.

Miller Street Bus Depot, Aston, 25th May 1971.

Aldridge Road, Great Barr, 24th June 1971.

Tyburn Road, Erdington, 1971.

Summer Lane, Newtown, August 1971.

Hagley Road, August 1971.

Maypole Lane, Kings Heath, 9th August 1971.

Duke of York, Key Hill/Hockley Hill, Hockley, 1971.

Aston Church Road, Saltley, 1971.

Queslett Road/Walsall Road, Great Barr, September 1971.

Princess Margaret meets Sir Felix Aylmer who spoke the first words on stage at the Old Rep and also at the opening of the New Rep, 20th October 1971.

Slade Road, with Marsh Hill on the right, Erdington, 21st October 1971.

# 1972

Raddlebarn Road/Dawlish Road, Selly Oak, 14th January 1972.

Brays Road, Sheldon, 28th February 1972.

St Clement's Church, Stuart Street/Nechells Park Road, Nechells, February 1972.

Strikers outside the West Midlands Gas Board Depot, Saltley, 9th February 1972.

Pershore Road, Stirchley, 28th March 1972.

Regina Drive, Perry Barr, 10th April 1972.

Joanne Dornin shows the petition she is organising to try and obtain a play area at Heybarnes Recreation Ground, Hay Mills, 11th April 1972.

Lucas's Sports Day, Witton, 1972.

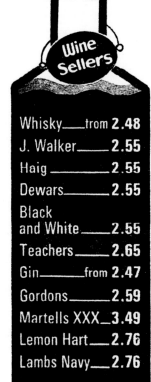
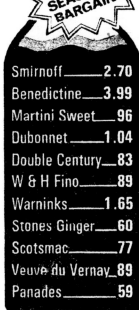

Camp Street, Bordesley, 8th June 1972.

Alexandra Road, Balsall Heath, 1972.

Gas Street Basin, 1972.

Ronald Road/Bordesley Green Road, 12th June 1972.

The Head Office of Birmingham Dairies, Island Road, Handsworth, 23rd June 1972.

Winson Green Road, with Heath Street on our left, 27th June 1972.

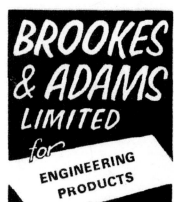

High Street, Erdington, September 1972.

The demolition men at work in Old Cross Street (facing Ryder Street), 4th October 1972.

High Street, with Castle Street on the immediate left, October 1972. Castle Street no longer exists.

Cherry Street, 2nd October 1972.

Islington Row, Five Ways, 1972.

Eden Place, between Victoria Square and Edmund Street, 1972.

Christine Hall and Anita Szolomicki end their all-night vigil by securing tickets for the Emerson, Lake and Palmer concert, at the Odeon, just three weeks away, 3rd November 1972.

Corporation Street, 16th December 1972.

One of the last working horses, "Mac", is seen with his owner, Alan Williams, Gas Street, 1973.

The junction of Cattell Road and Coventry Road, Small Heath, 1973.

Aldridge Road, Perry Barr, 31st January 1973.

Dawlish Road/Coronation Road, Selly Oak, 31st January 1973.

Eddystone Radio reception area, West Heath, 1973.

Solihull Lane, Hall Green, 8th February 1973.

Coventry Road, Small Heath, 16th March 1973.

Town Hall, 26th April 1973.

Moseley Road, Balsall Heath, April 1973.

## 'CENTURY' BAKERY CLOSES

### 20.5.73

A 100-YEAR-OLD Birmingham bakery merges into another company this weekend.

Hughleys shut down production at its High Street, Harborne, bakery on Friday and from tomorrow operates from Hardings bakery in Garretts Green.

Of the 135 Hughleys workers, 62 go to Hardings, 43 have been offered other jobs in consultation with the Department of Employment, and the others, mostly parttimers, lose their employment.

Cramped conditions and a planned road widening have caused the move.

The 38 Hughleys shops in Birmingham will keep the name, and will be served from Hardings. Both companies are part of the Rank Hovis McDougall group.

Hughleys, which makes crusty bread and cakes, began life at J. T. Vickers and Son Ltd. over 100 years ago, became Hughleys in 1959, and was taken over by RHM in 1963.

Workers organised a farewell party last night and baked a special goodbye cake.

Temple Row, 25th May 1973.

Soho Road, Handsworth, May 1973.

Woods, off The Croftway, Handsworth Wood, 1973.

The National Exhibition Centre starts to take shape, 1973.

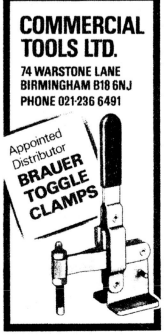

Graham Street, Hockley, 4th June 1973.

Ladypool Road/Turner Street, Sparkbrook, 5th July 1973.

41

Rear of Coleraine Road, Great Barr, July 1973.

A burst water main causes a spectacular display in Hagley Road, Edgbaston, 7th July 1973.

The Queen's Arms, Newhall Street/Charlotte Street, September 1973.

Harborne Council School, High Street, 1973.

Ombersley Road, leading down to Ladypool Road, Sparkbrook, 8th November 1973.

General Post Office, Victoria Square, 1973.

PHILLIPS-WINDSOR : On November 14, 1973, at Westminster Abbey, London. by His Grace the Lord Archbishop of Canterbury, Mark Anthony Peter, son of Major and Mrs. Peter Phillips, to Her Royal Highness Anne Elizabeth Alice Louise, Princess of the United Kingdom, daughter of Her Majesty the Queen and His Royal Highness Prince Philip, the Duke of Edinburgh.

Bennetts Hill/Waterloo Street, 1973.

Union Street, 26th November 1973.

# 1974

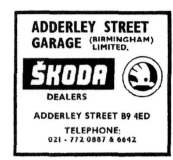

Whitepost Service Station, Bristol Road South, Rednal, 1974.

Shopkeepers promote their wares, Needless Alley, 1974.

Lozells Inn, Lozells Road, 12th January 1974.

Postmen at Erdington District Office,
Sutton New Road, 1974.

The Gracechurch Centre is underway,
Sutton Coldfield, 1974.

Lea Mason School, Lee Bank, February 1974.

G W & H Leaman, (builder's merchants), Sheaf Lane, Sheldon, 20th February 1974.

Pershore Avenue, Pershore Road, Selly Park, 1974.

Army disposal experts, with a bomb disposal robot, deal with yet another explosive device, Pinfold Street, 8th April 1974. This was just one of several attempted attacks on the city that led up to the notorious November incidents.

A bomb blast sale at Joan Barrie's fashion shop, The Rotunda, 16th July 1974.

The Futurist Cinema, John Bright Street, 1974.

The Gaumont cinema, Steelhouse Lane, 1974.

Edward Road, with Court Road in view,
Balsall Heath, 1974.

The Angel drinking fountain, Temple Row,
24th September 1974.

Smithfield Market, Moat Lane, c 1974.

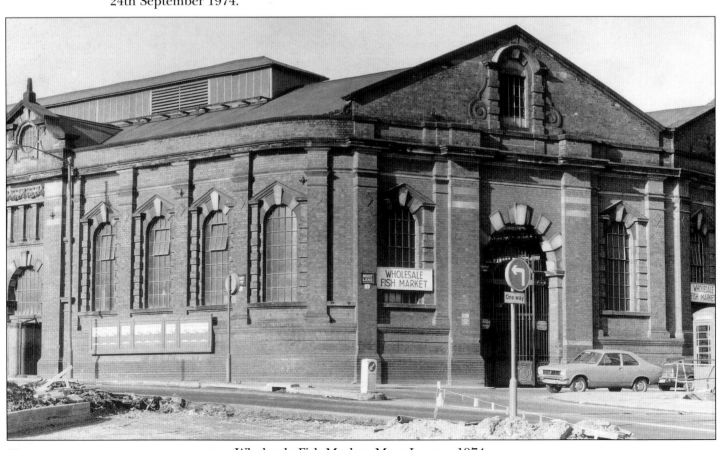

Wholesale Fish Market, Moat Lane, c 1974.

The Home Secretary, The Rt. Hon. Roy Jenkins, visits the scene of the pub bombings, New Street, 22nd November 1974.

Westminster Road/St Stephen's Road, Selly Oak, November 1974.

Nechells Primary School, Eliot Street, November 1974.

An open air service, conducted by the Bishop of Birmingham, the Rt. Rev. Laurence Brown, to pay respect to those killed or injured in the Birmingham bombings the week before, Ward End Park, 28th November 1974.

# 1975

## NEW CASTAWAYS
## THEATRE RESTAURANT

BRADFORD STREET. Tel.: 021-622 3670 and 3679.
COMING ATTRACTIONS
FRIDAY, JANUARY 24th (One Night Only)
FROM THE COMEDIANS
### CHARLIE WILLIAMS

WEEK COMMENCING SUNDAY, FEBRUARY 2nd. For One Week
TV AND FILM PERSONALITY
### NORMAN WISDOM

ONE NIGHT ONLY — MONDAY, MARCH 3rd
### THE SYD LAWRENCE ORCHESTRA

FURTHER ATTRACTIONS
### AYSHEA
(From the TV Programme with Take Off With Ayshea)

### THE FORMOST

### BROTHERHOOD OF MAN

AUGUST BANK HOLIDAY WEEK
### TONY CHRISTIE

Tickets on sale for all attractions any mid-week from 8 p.m. onward
at Reception.
MONDAY £1,000 TALENT CONTEST.
COME AND SEE OUR STARS OF TOMORROW

St Martins public house, Jamaica Row, 1975.

Tyburn Road, Erdington, January 1975.

Smithfield Market disappears, to reveal a new view of St Martin's, 28th February 1975.

The Old Crown public house, High Street/Heath Mill Lane, Deritend, c 1975.

57

Tyseley Motive Power Depot, Warwick Road, 18th March 1975.

Warwick Road, Greet, 18th March 1975.

Westley Road, Acocks Green, 15th April 1975.

Rear of Wolseley Street, Small Heath, 22nd April 1975.

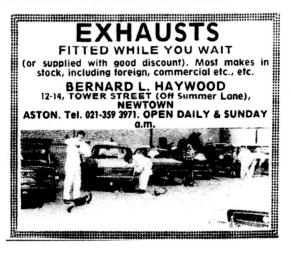
Forthcoming Attractions

# 1975

## MAY CONCERT

BOURNVILLE CONCERT HALL
SATURDAY, 17th MAY
7.30 p.m.

---

NORTHFIELD OPERATIC

# NOS

SOCIETY

---

**song**

**of**

**norway**

FEBRUARY
1976
PRODUCTION

CRESCENT THEATRE,
BIRMINGHAM

The Queen talks to Dr Kenneth Humphreys after opening the Mason College Centenary Exhibition, The University of Birmingham, 27th June 1975.

Singer, Amanda Lear, chats to BBC Radio Producer, Keith Ackrill, at a record company reception, 1975.

Albert Road, Stechford, 1975.

Pershore Road, Selly Park, 1975.

# 1976

Snow Hill, 1976.

St Chads Circus, 1976.

The Queen talks to the staff of the NEC on the opening day of the site, 2nd February 1976.

Acocks Green Shopping Centre, January 1976.

Temple Row, 1976.

Danny La Rue (centre) and the rest of the cast, promote their play, "Dead on Nine", Hippodrome, 30th March 1976.
The hearse is a nice touch!

Icknield Street, c 1976.

Barbara Henderson, of the Birmingham Mail, is shown one of the world's most expensive lighters by tobacconist, John Reynolds, 29th June 1976. The table lighter was valued at £32,000.

The Lord Mayor, Coun. Harold Powell, opens the play centre, in Robin Hood Crescent, Hall Green, 28th July 1976.

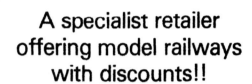

**BBC tv**

000704

invites you to

# 'POP at the Mill'

### ( AN OPEN AIR CONCERT )

---

Gates open 5.00 pm

Commence 5.30 pm

**ADMIT ONE**
(No children under 14 years)

Saturday, August 14th, 1976

THE LAWN

PEBBLE MILL ROAD

BIRMINGHAM

---

## BBC TELEVISION, BIRMINGHAM

---

*invites you to a recording of . .*

# "HEADLINE CHALLENGE"

### A NEWS QUIZ / PANEL GAME

in STUDIO A at PEBBLE MILL

**SATURDAY, 18th SEPTEMBER, 1976**

*You are asked to occupy your seat by 6 - 45 p.m.*

---

**ADMIT ONE**

16

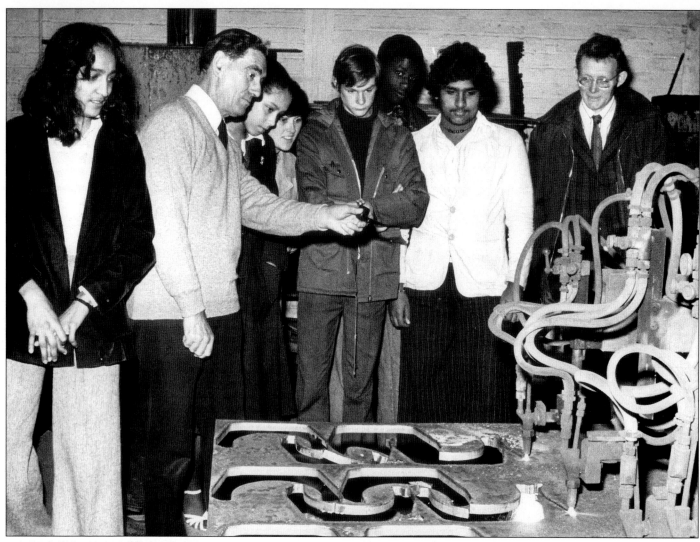

Youngsters take part in a Job Preparation Scheme, organised by Sparkhill Further Education Centre at Welforge Ltd., Halesowen, 15th October 1976. Commercial Manager, Roy Darnell, explains the manufacture of fabricated mining equipment, as the Director of the scheme, Peter Davie (right) looks on.

Pershore Road, Stirchley, c 1976.

St Stephen's Road/Milner Road, Selly Oak, 1977.

Lancaster Street, c 1977.

Sutton New Road, with Reservoir Road showing, Erdington, 1977.

High Street, Erdington, 18th January 1977.

Knightlow Road, Edgbaston, 1977.

Tyseley Station, 1977.

Snow Hill Station's last Stationmaster, George Smith, 1977. This was taken during the year the demolition of the station was completed.

Princess Anne greets the Villa players at the League Cup Final, Wembley, 12th March 1977. After two replays Villa beat Everton 3-2.

Aston Unity Cricket Club First XI, 1977.

Jim Peverelle, of Sutton Coldfield, skims across Pendigo Lake at rehearsals for a spectacular at the NEC, 1977.

Alcester Road, Moseley, 1977.

Oxhill Road/Avenue Road, Handsworth, c 1977.

Cherry Street, 1977.

SEVERNE ROAD SCHOOL

QUEEN'S SILVER JUBILEE PARTY

7th JUNE 1977

THE FOLLOWING PROGRAMME IS A GUIDE TO THE EVENTS FOR THE DAY

2.30p.m. - 3.00 p.m.

FANCY DRESS FOR THE YOUNGSTERS, ALSO FOR THE MUMS AND DADS.
THERE WILL ALSO BE A PRIZE FOR THE BEST JUBILEE PARTY HAT.

3.00 p.m. - 4.30 p.m.

CHILDREN'S GAMES, SPORTS FOR ALL, FOR WHICH PRIZES WILL BE GIVEN.

4.30 p.m. - 5.30 p.m.

CHILDREN'S TEA.

5.30 p.m. - 7.00 p.m.

CHILDREN'S ENTERTAINMENTS AND GAMES, DANCING ETC.,

7.00 p.m. - 10.30 approx.

DANCING TO A DISCO AND BUFFET.

BADGES

ALL CHILDREN AND TEENAGERS WILL BE GIVEN A BADGE TO WEAR ON THE
DAY - PLEASE MAKE SURE THESE ARE WORN, SO THAT WE CAN AVOID ANY
GATE CRASHERS.

SOUVENIRS

THESE WILL BE PRESENTED DURING THE EVENING.

Rowheath Farm, Selly Oak Road, Kings Norton, 1977.

Rachel England is chosen as West Heath's Carnival Princess, 21st June 1977.

Birmingham greets the Queen, as part of her
Silver Jubilee celebrations, Victoria Square and
Chamberlain Place, 27th July 1977.

Silver Jubilee celebrations, Meridan Way, Kingshurst,
27th July 1977.

Kings Norton's cryer, Ivor Cooke,
commemorates the Queen's Silver Jubilee,
Saracen's Head.

Silver Jubilee celebrations, Kings Norton Green.

Silver Jubilee celebrations in Windsor Road, Stirchley.

Silver Jubilee Fancy Dress Party, Fox Hollies Inn,
Acocks Green.

Karen Smith is the choice as this year's Birmingham Rag Queen, Aston University, October 1977.

Frank Riego, Manager of the Plaza, arrives at work only to find that the cinema is up for sale, Stockland Green, 17th November 1977.

Ronnie Hilton and Barbara Windsor can hardly wait for the opening night of "Aladdin",
Alexandra Theatre, 21st December 1977.

Stars of TV's "Robin's Nest", Richard O'Sullivan and Tessa Wyatt, along with other cast members, break off from
rehearsals for "Cinderella", Hippodrome, 21st December 1977.

# 1978

Angry parents barricade the road to draw attention to the dangers of speeding motorists, Barrows Road, Sparkbrook, 1978.

Children from Castle Vale School brush up on their Russian before setting off behind the Iron Curtain, 7th February 1978.

Hay Mills Police Station, Coventry Road, c 1978.

Small Heath Police Station, Coventry Road, 1978.

W Canning & Co. Ltd. football team, 1978.

Father and son, Harold and Norman Benson, man their radio and
television shop in Kings Road, Hay Mills, 1978.

Regent Park Road, Small Heath, c 1978.

Regent Park Road/Coventry Road, Small Heath, c 1978.

Factory units, Heaton Street, Hockley, 1978.

Pershore Road, Stirchley, 1978.

Nechells Park Road/Crompton Road, Nechells, c 1978.

The junction of Hill Street and Station Street, c 1978.

The Wholesale Horticultural Market, 1978.

Peter Braddock brings the jungle to Cotteridge!
The Treasure Trove, Pershore Road, 1978.

A workman sharpens a circular saw blade with a file, Atkin & Sons Ltd.,
Bradford Street, 1978. The firm's founder, Aeron Atkin, walked from
Sheffield to Birmingham carrying his tools on his back in 1760.
The firm closed down in 1983.

A runaway goods train plunges down the embankment, Handsworth New Road, Winson Green, 8th July 1978.

The fun of building a bonfire for the children from Vivian Road, Harborne, November 1978.

# 1979

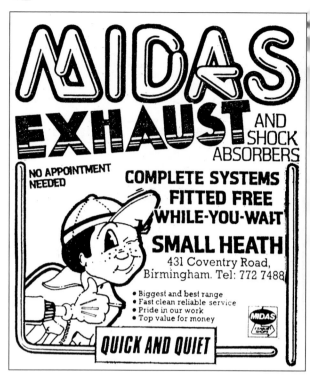

American actor, Telly Savalas (of "Kojak" fame) has recorded the narration for a documentary called, "Telly Savalas Looks at Birmingham", 1979.

Comedian Larry Grayson, flanked by members of the Great Barr Judo Club, at an Open Day at George Heath Motors, Coventry Road, Small Heath, 1979.

Anita Harris, Tommy Trinder and Frankie Howerd make a summer trip to the Alexandra Theatre to promote their Christmas Panto, "Robinson Crusoe", 13th July 1979

The planned airport expansion leads to a protest, Elmdon, 1st August 1979.

Brian Matthews, Chairman of Small Heath Local History Society, raises his hat in salute as he prepares to mark part of Small Heath Park's centenary celebrations, 20th August 1979.

A celebratory toast by the workmen who had just built a show house in six days for the Evening Mail Midlands' Ideal Home Exhibition, Bingley Hall, 6th September 1979.

Capitol Cinema, just prior to its conversion into a three screen cinema, Alum Rock Road, Ward End. 14th September 1979.

Garrison Lane/Barwell Road, Bordesley Green, 1979.

The Lord Mayor, Coun. Edward Hanson, has just unveiled a Civic Society Plaque marking the site of the original General Hospital, in Summer Lane, 18th October 1979.

Coventry Road, South Yardley, c 1979.

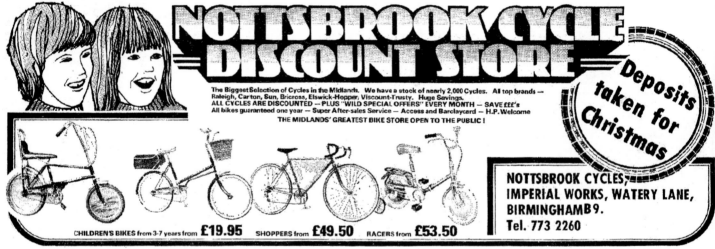

A carol concert given by ambulance controllers at St Mary's Hospice, Selly Oak, 23rd December 1979.
They had also agreed to make a regular contribution, through their social club funds, to the hospice.

Back Cover: Building workers stage a demonstration for better pay on the shoulders of King Kong, Bull Ring Shopping Centre, 14th July 1972.

## ACKNOWLEDGEMENTS
### (for providing photographs, encouragement and numerous other favours)

Barbara Ackrill; Keith Ackrill; Peter Ashlington; Norman Bailey; The Birmingham City Council Dept. of Planning and Architecture; The Birmingham Post and Mail Ltd.; Peter Braddock; John and Masie Brown; Roy Dillon; Paula Earle; Ray Green; Joyce Hargreaves; Phil Haycock; Doug Hobson; Brenda Johnson; Dave, Thelma and Tom Jones; Royston Kemp; Sylvia Manton; Brian Matthews; Dennis Moore; George Peace; Gertrude and Alan Peters; Brian Pinkerton; Dave Robinson; Geoffrey Round; Keith Shakespeare; Joan Ward; Len Thompson; Rosemary Wilkes; Ken Windsor.

Please forgive any possible omissions. Every effort has been made to include all organisations and individuals involved in the book.

John and Hilda England, two of the city's longest-serving teachers, prepare to say goodbye to some of their pupils, 15th July 1971. Between them they had notched up 80 years of teaching. John was saying goodbye to Nelson School and Hilda was leaving World's End Primary School.